FURRY PURRY FRIENDS

THE DEFINITIVE GUIDE TO TUXEDO CATS AS PETS:

THE BRIEF GUIDE TO TUXEDO CATS - INCLUDING THE GROOMING, BREEDING AND CARING FOR EVERY OWNER.

Wendy Davis

D1546016

Table of Contents

Introduction

It seems that everybody loves Tuxedo cats. These big, lovable giants of the cat world are the first natural breed to emerge from the regions of northern America, and while their origins are shrouded in mystery, nobody has any doubts as to the gentleness, affection, and loyalty of these big cats.

Facts About Tuxedo Cats

In general, queens are good mothers, and they will know instinctively how to take care of their young. Allow her to settle herself and her litter in peace and without many interruptions, and without handling them for the first 24-48 hours after birth, you are allowing the queen to bond with her newborns in a peaceful and nurturing environment.

The queen will take care of pretty much everything, from nursing them, cleaning and grooming them, and even teaching them to use the litter box. Human intervention only comes in when checking them, weighing the kittens, and gentle handling for early socialization. It is not advisable, however, to take them away from their mother for prolonged periods of time as this may stress out both the mother and the kittens.

You should expect a weight gain of at least 10 grams per day. If it does not seem like the kittens are gaining much weight at all, it probably means that the mother is not producing enough milk. It is important to give her a calcium-rich diet while she is lactating, to give her the energy and the necessary nutrients to feed her young ones. Consult with your veterinarian if she does not seem to be eating well, or if any of her milk glands appear swollen. On the other hand, if any of the kittens seem cold or does not seem to be gaining any weight, bring the kitten to the veterinarian immediately.

Weaning starts at around 4 weeks. By this time, you can start providing them with high quality kitten kibbles soaked or moistened with water or kitten formula. You can encourage them to try the food by placing some on their lips and positioning them near the bowl. For the next two weeks, allow them free choice of nursing or prepared food while handling them gently and regularly as much as possible. This will help them gain both human and cat social skills within a positive environment.

The kittens should be fully weaned at around 6 to 8 weeks. At around this time, you can begin regulating the mother's diet in order to help her milk supply to dry up. Slowly decrease her food and water portions each day, until she is back to her pre-pregnancy diet levels. If she seems to have lost weight during the pregnancy and lactation period, adjust her food intake accordingly.

Summary of Tuxedo Cat Facts

Pedigree: unknown

Breed Size: medium to large

Weight: average 8 to 18 lbs. (3.6 to 8.2 kg.)

Body Type: large body, robust bone structure, well-muscled

Coat Length: uneven coat length; short on the head and shoulders, gradually increasing in length along the back and sides, ending in full britches, long, shaggy belly fur, and full, long and flowing fur along the tail.

Coat Texture: soft but with body, falling smoothly and lies close to the body

Eyes: eyes are large, with a slight oblique setting

Ears: large, wide at the base, moderately pointed and well-tufted

Tail: long, wide at the base and tapering, with full, long and flowing fur

Temperament: friendly, affectionate, loving, loyal and goofy

Strangers: cautious with strangers, though never mean or shy

Children: kind, playful, and very good with children

Other Pets: gets along with dogs and most other pets

Exercise Needs: provide adequate exercise and mental stimulation, such as perches, adequate running room, and sufficient playtime

Health Conditions: generally healthy but prone to some hereditary conditions such as Feline Hypertrophic Cardiomyopathy (HCM), Spinal Muscular Atrophy (SMA), Hip Dysplasia (HD), and Polycystic Kidney Disease (PKD)

Lifespan: average 9 to 13 years

Chapter One: Understanding Tuxedo Cats

After a brief overview of the typical traits of the Tuxedo Cat, the theories of its origins, and a brief history of its stint as a show cat, we now turn to some of the more practical aspects of cat ownership: their temperament, whether you need a license, the costs of purchasing and keeping a Tuxedo, and the pros and cons of this breed. This will enable you to judge whether your lifestyle and home is a fit for this breed, and whether you should be looking further into purchasing one of your own.

Do You Need a License?

While there are no federal requirements in the United States for licensing cat owners, local states may have specific regulations governing pet ownership. This varies depending on your area or region, so it is always best to check with your local municipality regarding the pertinent laws in force in your state.

A cat licensing program is usually geared towards curbing cat overpopulation, and you will find that a license for neutered cats is cheaper than that for cats who are intact. These licenses are usually required to be renewed annually.

Even if your state does not require you to get a license for your cat, it is still a good idea to have them microchipped. This is actually a good idea for cats - even if they are properly licensed. The reason is that a license tag is usually attached to a collar, and sometimes those collars come off. Microchipping/ tattooing and registering ensures that you can still be identified as the registered owner even without the cat's license tags.

Be aware that in states which require cat licenses, the laws also apply to indoor cats, even if they are already microchipped. Failure to license a cat can result in a fine. Every cat of a certain age, whether kept indoors or allowed outdoors, is required to be licensed and registered in certain states. You'll never know when this comes in handy as there are various circumstances - whether foreseen or unforeseen - which can cause a separation between a cat and its owner.

Do Tuxedo Cats Get Along with Other Pets?

Tuxedo cats are a gentle and affectionate bunch, and they get along well with children and other household pets. But be advised that Tuxedos were bred to be mousers - their original work. You'll never have to fear having a mouse wandering in your home if you have a Tuxedo! That said, while Tuxedos generally get along well with other pets such as dogs and other cats, you might want to exercise due caution if you also have smaller pets such as birds, mice, or hamsters. There have been reports of Tuxedos coexisting nicely with smaller animals, but you will never truly remove their instinctive predator instinct. Caution and proper supervision is always advised.

How Many Tuxedo Cats Should You Keep?

It is up to you, as the prospective cat owner, how many Tuxedo cats you wish to keep. If you have the space for them, are able to afford their upkeep, and are willing to put in the energy and care that is required in keeping more than one cat, then by all means do so!

There are, however, some additional considerations for you to keep in mind as you consider bringing in more than one Tuxedo into your home:

- There might be some dominance displays between or among your cats, so you will likely have to provide multiple pet beds, food and water bowls, and even litter boxes. Yes, some cats dislike having to go in a box where other cats have already done their business. Allowing each cat their own space and things will reduce much of the resulting confusion and chaos that can ensue.

- Be particularly wary of bringing together a male and female cat. Unless you are planning to breed - and have the knowledge and resources to do so - then please do the responsible thing and neuter your cats. Things might get particularly rowdy when your female cat reaches her age of first heat. Having a bunch of tom cats hanging around outside your house might be bad enough, and mating displays between your male and female cat might, at the very least, become embarrassing. But having your female cat birthing one litter after another will likely not become more endearing with the next unexpected and unplanned litter!

Chapter Two: Things to Know Before Getting a Tuxedo Cat

How Much Does It Cost to Keep a Tuxedo Cat?

It is very easy to underestimate the cost and upkeep of keeping a Tuxedo - many people tend not to look beyond the initial purchase price, and generally have a vague idea of what pet food might cost. Before you even think of getting a Tuxedo - you have to understand that they will require some recurring expenses that can quickly add up unless you have budgeted properly.

Expect to shell out more during your first year of pet ownership, as you will be purchasing the kitten as well as most of the tools, equipment and pet accessories you will be needing during your first year. Add the expenses of neutering or spaying, and the initial costs, including their purchase price, can vary. Getting a cat from a shelter will cost a lot less than purchasing a kitten from a reputable breeder with all the required papers and a proud pedigree. As a general range, however, you can probably expect to shell out some $400-1,000 (£308.88-772.2) for a purebred Tuxedo. Additional initial costs include:

- Pet equipment and accessories such as a bed, collar, food and water bowls, grooming accessories, and a good range of cat toys. A good estimate for this is about $250 (£193.05)
- The costs of microchipping your cat can range from around $20-25 (£15.44-19.31).
- Spaying or Neutering, with Veterinarian fees can average anywhere from $130-170 (£100.39-131.27)

- Your cat may come to you already having received their initial vaccinations. Some additional vaccinations might be required, however, and it is a good idea to budged around $50 (£38.61) for this.

These initial costs would be in addition to the annual costs of food, cat litter, regular de-worming, flea treatments, veterinarian fees, pet insurance (when applicable), and grooming expenses. An estimated breakdown of these annual expenses are as follows:

- Food: $250-310 (£193.05-239.38)
- Cat Litter: $75-150 (£57.92-115.83)
- Worming: $50-75 (£38.61-57.92)
- Flea Treatment: $75 (£57.92)
- Veterinarian fees: $50-65 (£38.61-50.19)
- Insurance: $95-235 (£73.36-181.47)
- Grooming and other miscellaneous expenses: $250-645 (£193.05-498.07)

Keep in mind that these are just wide-margin estimates, and the moneywise cat owner can certainly find ways and means of saving. Costs may also vary depending on your location, your selection of pet products, and the rates of veterinary services in your area. But some experts agree that a cat owner should have an emergency pet fund of at least $1,000 set aside for unforeseen emergencies - which will likely be medical in nature, just in case.

A breakdown of these expenses is shown in the table below:

Item	Initial Costs	Annual Costs
Initial Purchase Price	$400-1,000 (£308.88-772.2)	
Pet Equipment and Accessories	$250 (£193.05)	
Microchipping	$20-25 (£15.44-19.31)	
Food		$250-310 (£193.05-239.38)
Cat Litter		$75-150 (£57.92-115.83)
Veterinarian Fees, Spaying or Neutering	$130-170 (£100.39-131.27)	
Vaccinations	$50 (£38.61)	
Worming		$50-75 (£38.61-57.92)
Flea Treatment		$75 (£57.92)
Veterinarian Fees		$50-65 (£38.61-50.19)
Insurance		$95-235 (£73.36-181.47)
Grooming and other miscellaneous expenses		$250-645 (£193.05-498.07)

*Costs may vary depending on location

**U.K. prices based on an estimated exchange of $1 = £0.77

What are the Pros and Cons of Tuxedo Cats?

To summarize, below is a list of the pros and cons of keeping a Tuxedo cat. If you are still undecided about whether or not this is the right breed for you, read on. A Tuxedo cat is like any other cat, but certainly bigger in so many ways. Some of these traits might be good for some, and some of their quirks might need some level of tolerance for some pet owners. The following lists should serve as a general guide on your decision as to whether the Tuxedo is the right cat breed for you:

Pros of the Tuxedo Cat Breed

- Loyal
- Laid-back and low maintenance
- Clownish and playful
- Generally healthy with few breed-specific health conditions
- Depending on your preference and living space, these are big sized cats - desirable for some, though maybe not for others
- Intelligent and trainable
- A beautiful breed, but low maintenance in terms of coat grooming
- A distinctive trill or chirp that can be delightful to hear

Cons of the Tuxedo Cat Breed

- With that abundance of long hair, they do require regular grooming. Otherwise, they can shed a lot, and their hair can get matted or tangled

- The grooming requirements may require the additional bath as some of their poop may get on the abundance of hair on their furry tails and rear ends
- Their large size does require sufficient space - especially enough running room for when they are feeling playful. If you have a very small apartment or living space, your cat might not be able to thrive as it cannot exercise or run around properly

Chapter Three: Purchasing Your Tuxedo Cat

After seeing an overview of the practical aspects of what it means to add a Tuxedo cat to your household, and your heart is still set on getting one for a pet, the next thing to do is to set out finding the right cat for you. There are many options available to prospective pet owners: rescuing cats from a shelter should definitely be an option as you will literally be rescuing cats in need of a good home. Alternatively, you can look into getting one from a reputable breeder. If you do this right, you will be assured that you are getting a healthy cat from a good pedigree, who has undergone the proper health and medical checks. Towards the end of the chapter, we will look into the more practical aspects of preparing your home for the arrival of your new family member.

Where Can You Buy Tuxedo Cats?

The combination of cats' natural fecundity, their sheer numbers, and their tendency to wander has resulted in the unfortunate situation prevalent today of lots of homeless and semi-feral cats and kittens wandering around the world over. Many owners end up adopting stray kittens only later to learn that these are actually Tuxedos, or at least have some Tuxedo blood in their pedigree.

If you wish to help alleviate this state of affairs, you might want to consider opening up your home to one of these lost cats. There are many rescues the world over for both dogs and cats, many of them breed-specific. You can search online for one nearest you, or you can use the following list as a starting point in locating the nearest Tuxedo rescue in your area:

As an alternative, you can check out the websites of some international or internarial cat organizations that recognize the Tuxedo as a breed. They usually carry a list of cat shelters in various areas or regions, and they also carry a list of reputable breeders who have undergone intensive screening to meet with the association's standards.

How to Choose a Reputable Tuxedo Cat Breeder

If you choose to purchase your cat from a breeder, it pays to know how to choose a reputable breeder. This is important because there are far too many breeders out there who are only in it for the money, not the cat's best interests. On the negative side, you might end up with a maladjusted or poorly socialized cat, whose parents have not been screened for the genetic illnesses to which Tuxedos are prone to. For the good money, you are shelling out to these breeders, you should at least expect some sort of assurance that the risks of any illnesses or diseases have been kept to a minimum.

So how do you go about choosing a reputable breeder? A good first step is to look at the listings of breeders among the various cat organizations that recognize the Tuxedo as a breed, such as the TICA, the CFA, or the MBCFA. You can look for these listings online, or alternatively, you can attend one of the cat shows being held by these groups. Many of those showing their cats are breeders, so right during the show you can already determine for yourself how much care and attention they give to their Tuxedos. It is probably a safe bet that such enthusiasm for the breed extends to their breeding programs.

In addition, breeders are not listed by these organizations randomly. Their catteries usually go through regular screening, and they will not be listed unless they meet the organization's standards.

Begin reaching out, either introducing yourself in person during the show, or contacting them online. You must first start a conversation regarding Tuxedos, and this is the perfect chance for you to ask questions about the breed, just to make doubly sure that this breed really is the right cat for you. A reputable breeder will usually be just as enthusiastic in discussing many of the Tuxedo's characteristics, needs, and quirks.

You can then ask to visit their cattery, which any good breeder will only be too happy to show you. You can then judge for yourself how clean the queen and the kittens are, whether they are well-fed and healthy, and how their surroundings are maintained. Ask about their feeding, health and early socialization. But be prepared to answer questions yourself. Any responsible breeder is just as interested in placing their kittens with responsible owners as you are in getting a good and healthy kitten. With proper communication, you might find yourself building a good relationship with a person who is a good source to ask about any questions you might have about your cat in the future.

When you are satisfied, you are probably going to put down a deposit for your future Tuxedo. Do this, and settle in to wait.

As a final note, it is best to avoid purchasing your cats from your local pet stores. The truth is that no reputable breeder will even consider placing their kittens in those little cages, to be displayed at the shop windows. No matter how cute they may look from across the glass windows, you simply cannot be sure about the cat's or the kitten's background and breeding history. Better to adopt from a rescue, than paying for, and inadvertently supporting, disreputable breeders who mass produce litters and sell to stores.

Tips for Selecting a Healthy Tuxedo Kitten

Once you have selected a good and reputable Tuxedo breeder, half of the job is already done. You can at least rest assured that the entire litter has been prepared for in the same way: health checks and screenings for both the stud and the queen, and a nurturing and healthy environment where the kittens were bed, born, and grew up in.

Now all that is left is to pick your kitten. Rest assured by this point that whichever kitten you pick; you are getting one that is as healthy as all the others. Perhaps the only real difference now is in the traits and characteristics that are unique for each cat.

Remember that a kitten should not be completely separated from its mother until it is at least 10 weeks of age. Some breeders wait until the kittens are at least 12 weeks before handing them over to the new owners. By this time, they should be fully weaned and are capable of living apart from their mother.

The kitten should be well-socialized, which means that it is naturally playful and curious, even with you, a stranger - though perhaps you can make allowance for some timidity and cautiousness at first. Watch out for possible signs of sickness, such as diarrhea, a stuffy nose, sticky eyes, or unnatural thinness. A kitten should be healthy, with clear eyes and nose, the beginnings of a luxurious coat, and suitably plump and cute.

This means that they have a healthy appetite, are well-socialized, and will be happy to explore the rest of the world with you!

Preparing Your Home

It is generally a good idea to confine your kitten to one room in the beginning - a place where everything he needs is within easy reach: his bed, his litter, his water and food bowls, and enough toys at his disposal. Eventually, however, you can reasonably expect that they will have access to your entire home. Their natural curiosity almost demands a complete inspection of their new house. So, it is always a good idea to prepare your home beforehand, to kitten-proof it (which is not unlike baby-proofing your home) so that the kitten's natural curiosity will not lead them to dangerous antics or explorations.

There can be as many dangers inside the home, as there are outside. Here are some tips for kitten-proofing your home:

- Put away any loose strings of any kind. Ribbons, dental floss, yarn - kittens love to play with them, which means they might eventually swallow them. This is potentially hazardous to your kitten, so keep those lovely bits of string secure in a high place.

- Secure or tuck away electrical cords, curtains, and cords. A loose electrical cord can electrocute your kitten, and other loose cords can strangle them even as they play. On the other hand, you might have kittens climbing up floor-length curtains to get to the top. It's probably a good idea to flip those curtains over the rods - at least for the first few months.

- Beware that kittens also do love to nibble: so, keep away plants, medication, garbage, cleaning supplies, and even your food.

- Secure water containers with tight lids to prevent accidental drowning - Tuxedos are noted for loving water, but this is potentially dangerous for kittens that venture into deep containers of water. For that matter, it's probably a good idea to put the toilet seat down.

- Secure the screens on your door and windows. Yes, cats and kittens can be escape artists, and unless you are watching them 24-7, an open door can prove to be too much of a curiosity. Don't allow those little kittens outdoors unsupervised - remember that the world is pretty dangerous for tiny kittens, and you don't want to run the risk of having them be run over by a car, climbing a tree they can't get out of, of sometimes even being kidnapped! Take all necessary precautions as you would with a child - which, essentially, your kittens are.

- Those little kittens certainly have the capacity of getting into tight spots you couldn't have imagined. So, it's always a good idea to check your appliances before turning them on: such as the washing machine and dryer. Sometimes they can hide or curl up beneath a recliner or a sofa. You are probably going to have to watch your step for the first few months as the kittens explore their new home and are liable to get underfoot much of the time!

Chapter Four: Caring for Your New Tuxedo

Often nicknamed the "gentle giant," Tuxedos are good pets for first time cat owners. They are an adaptable breed, gentle, kind, affectionate, loyal, and in terms of needs and attention, he isn't high maintenance. They have a comical side to them that they retain even into adulthood. And it won't really take much effort to keep them happy. They are good-natured cats, happy to receive attention when you give it, is patient with his owners and the rest of his family, and tolerant even of the more attention-seeking pets you may have.

Tuxedo cat owners are always delighted to do what they can to keep their cat healthy - that is because they demand so little. In this chapter, you can learn more about some of the things that this breed will appreciate in his new home - from enough running space, sufficient playtime, and the occasional venture out of doors.

Habitat and Exercise Requirements for Tuxedo Cats

Because the Tuxedo is a large cat, this breed does need some exercise. Even if it is kept mainly as an indoors cat, they will still need some form of exercise through which they can burn their energy and thus keep from becoming overweight. If you have a yard, be sure to provide sufficient fencing or outdoor cat enclosures, especially if your Tuxedo is still a kitten. Whether or not you keep your cat as an indoor or outdoor cat is an owner's choice, but be sure you make this decision with the best interests of your cat in mind. Are your streets safe? Many kittens are prone to vehicular accidents, and of course, the more expensive breeds can simply be stolen. All things considered, experts are in agreement that cats do not really need to be outside. In this day and age, doing so might actually shorten their lifespan considerably.

That said, many owners have been able to successfully keep a Tuxedo as a purely indoor cat. Occasionally, you might want to bring him outside for a walk on a harness and leash, and done often enough, this can provide your cat with enough physical and mental stimulation to keep them happy and healthy.

Don't forget to make your home conducive for your new pet, as well. As they mature, they will take up a lot of space - and you need to give them a special place in your home which they can call your own. Tuxedos are not lap cats - their size will make this quite awkward. But they do like to stay close to their owners. Their expressions of loyalty and devotion are, in fact, not unlike that manifested by dogs. They will wait at the door for when you arrive, and should you be sitting at your desk working, there's nothing they like better than curling up beside your feet to keep you company. Nothing makes them happier than to have you reach over occasionally to give them an occasional pat or stroke.

As an alternative to letting cats outside, you can probably provide them with enough space in the home that is theirs completely. Equip this space with a good cat bed, enough toys to keep them occupied, a scratching post, high resting places, and enough nooks and crannies where they can play hide. Needless to say, clean food and water bowls, and a clean litter completes their necessary environment.

The rest of it is really up to you and how you interact with your Tuxedo on a day-to-day basis. They might not demand attention, but they do require regular displays of affection and attention. And keep their bowls, litter and bed clean. As noted in a later chapter, socialization is a continuous process, and it keeps your cat from being alienated and unhappy. At the extreme, an unhappy cat may eventually grow feral if kept in an inappropriate and unfulfilling environment. Or they may simply lose their affection for you if you don't show them enough attention and affection.

Toys and Accessories for Tuxedo Cats

For a large and dignified breed, the Tuxedo is oddly clownish and a bit of a goofball, even until they mature. But this just makes them more endearing to most pet owners.

It bears remembering, however, that like most cats, Tuxedos love to play. While you might eventually gather a good selection of toys during the cat's lifetime, he might show marked preference for some toys over others, then changes his preferences over time. Each cat is unique in this, so it is as well to provide them with a good selection of toys and accessories to keep them happy.

Many times, cats will find enough play in the most random things. But it is always a good idea to provide them with toys that are theirs alone, as it would also be an expression of how special they are to you. Below are some ideas for cat toys and other cat accessories you can experiment with to see which would engage your Tuxedo's interests and attention:

- perches
- scratching posts

- a variety of toys such as ping pong balls, cardboard boxes, toy mice, bird feather teaser, catnip, laser, or anything another simple thing the can play with.

Chapter Five: Meeting Your Tuxedo Cat's Nutritional Needs

Any good and responsible cat owner wants to give their Tuxedo the best, and that includes food! These days, however, the choices are so unlimited and varying, with widely diverging expert opinions, that it can get confusing.

While not endorsing any specific brand, or feeding program, this chapter aims to encapsulate some of the basic principles on the do's and don'ts's of feeding your cat. The process of finding the right cat food will likely be a journey for you as the owner, since even these guidelines will have to be adjusted to your own pet's preferences and reactions to their food, which means that you will still need to adjust accordingly. The best feedback you can get for what food and feeding regimen works best for your Tuxedo comes your cat himself. Does he eat heartily or does his appetite seem low? Does he have enough energy each day? Is he gaining too much weight? Does he seem lethargic and low on energy?

Try not to make any drastic changes in your cat's diet. If you do want to transition to something else, make the change gradually to get his stomach used to the idea of the new food. This way, you can also monitor any changes that might show with the new diet.

The Nutritional Needs of Cats

We'll try to make this section as painless as possible. Below is a breakdown of some guidelines regarding cat nutrition:

- Cats are obligate carnivores. This means that meat needs to be the main component of their diet. It shouldn't be too difficult to comprehend: remember that cats chase mice? In a natural setting, cats will gravitate towards raw meat whenever possible, and they have evolved as predators of smaller prey. Some owners swear by a raw meat diet, with additional natural supplements for nutrients that they cannot get from meat, such as vitamins A, B, C, D, and E, and calcium. Others look for high quality meat-based cat food, with the main component being either chicken, chicken meal, or fish meal.

- Avoid chicken by-products and chicken by-product meal. Mainly, these are composed of the rendered parts of the chicken, such as the head, feet, viscera, necks, undeveloped eggs, and intestines. While cats are natural carnivores, not even a cat in the wild can survive on by-products alone. They will need good, quality meat, and they will not be able to get enough nutritional value from these meat by-products alone.

- Avoid corn meal, corn gluten meal, and wheat gluten. These are cheap fillers, and are also highly allergenic, which can cause a cat to develop Irritable Bowel Syndrome or even induce vomiting. In any form, these ingredients are difficult for a cat to digest, so steer clear!

- Good grains for a cat include rice, rice flour, barley, barley flour, or milled barley. Higher quality cat food typically includes these ingredients as a good source of carbohydrates. Make sure that these are secondary ingredients in any cat food, however. Protein from meats should still be the main ingredient.

- Your Tuxedo cat should always have a readily available source of clean drinking water which he can reach at any hour of the day.

- Be on the lookout for these additional nutrients on the label, which are also necessary for your cat's daily diet: calcium, phosphorous, vitamin c, and taurine

How to Select a High-Quality Cat Food Brand

You are probably going to rotate your cat food choices over time, not only to ensure that a cat gets the best possible nutrition from both canned and dry food, while also keeping a variety of food choices available for your cat so that he doesn't get bored. Rotating food choices, and in fact mixing canned and dry food is recommended by many nutritionists to give your cat a more balanced diet.

But how do you choose among the varied options of cat food currently available? First of all, do your homework. While we cannot provide specific feedback on the different brands that are commercially available, there are many helpful forums and product reviews online of cat lovers and their feedback regarding certain cat food products. Asking questions and networking among the different cat owners you meet at cat shows, at the vet, your breeder, or friends who are also cat owners, can give you very real feedback regarding actual effects or quality of specific cat food brands. Keep an open mind, but be discerning. Read, and keep abreast of new developments in the industry. There are always new products coming on the market, so part of the journey is staying informed.

In addition, you are going to have to learn how to read the label of the selection of cat food available to you. First of all, look for one that meets or exceeds AAFCO standards. And don't forget to check the expiration date on the box.

Secondly, look for age-appropriate cat food. Depending on which stage of life your cat is in, different formulations of cat food are specifically targeted to meet the nutritional needs of your cat at a specific age. Hence, choose between kitten, adult, or senior cat food.

And as noted above, look for meat-based cat food as much as possible. You can tell the primary components of any cat food by which ingredients are listed first - and these should include the following:

- Protein from meat sources such as fish, poultry, or beef
- Taurine
- Vitamins, minerals, enzymes, fatty acids
- Water

Avoid fillers such as corn, wheat, cornmeal, by products, added sugars, and artificial or chemical preservatives such as BHA, BHT, ethoxyquin, and propyl gallate.

Tips for Feeding Your Tuxedo Cat

Feeding Tuxedos are not noticeably different from feeding most other cats. Your cat's unique quirks will determine, to a large extent, the type of feeding method you will use. Some cats are finicky eaters, and the free feeding method should work well with this type of cat. Basically, you leave them food in the bowl which they can return to any time during the day when they feel hungry. This is actually recommended for kittens who will likely space out their feeding in small portions throughout the day. But this also limits your options when it comes to the type of food you give them - dry food is best since wet food, or even raw meat, will not keep if left out for too long in the open air.

And yet this is probably the best and only option for people whose lifestyles keep them out of the house more often than not. Free feeding at least ensures that your cat does not go hungry during the day when you are away. But what to do when you have a cat who is dangerously close to obesity?

You might want to consider having someone feed your cat for you throughout the day. Alternatively, there are mechanical food bowls that can be set to feed small portions at specific times throughout a day.

Another feeding method - which has been openly acknowledged as the healthier option - is scheduled feedings with controlled portions. Scheduled feeding time also allows your cat to learn some discipline, especially if you choose to take away their food bowls after their schedule is up. This teaches them that in order to feed well, they have to eat all the contents of their bowl - thus ensuring that they are getting their proper nutrition, while also keeping their food and their food bowls clean and fresh, as opposed to food that is left out in the open for too long. Others, however, choose to measure out the food portions and leave it for the cat to eat at his own pace. This might be the more feasible option for you if you have an extremely finicky cat that prefers to eat sparingly, no matter if you take their bowls away after some time.

Always remember to provide them with clean and fresh drinking water that they can easily get to throughout the day. Clean their food and water bowls daily, and don't disturb them when they are eating. Again, be attentive to your cat and his state of health, adjusting your choice of food, his daily portions, and his unique feeding preferences.

Dangerous Foods to Avoid

Not all people foods are safe for your cats to eat. Fact is, some of them can be downright dangerous! Below is a list of some of dangerous foods you should avoid giving your cat. Should your Tuxedo ingest any of the following, call the Pet Poison Control hotline right away at (888) 426 – 4435.

- Alcohol
- Apple seeds
- Avocado
- Candy and gum
- Cherry pits
- Chives
- Chocolate
- Caffeine
- Fat trimmings and bones
- Garlic
- Grapes/raisins
- Hops
- Macadamia nuts
- Milk and other dairy products
- Mold
- Mushrooms
- Mustard seeds
- Onions/leeks
- Peach pits
- Potato leaves/stems
- Raw eggs

- Rhubarb leaves
- Tea
- Tomato leaves/stems
- Tuna
- Walnuts
- Xylitol
- Yeast dough

Chapter Six: Training Your Tuxedo Cat

Cats have good memories, and the Tuxedo cat, in particular, is an intelligent breed that can certainly be taught a trick or two! Tuxedos are sometimes called the dogs of the cat world, and these gentle giants are not too dignified for learned behavior. Of course, in training a Tuxedo cat, you must start with the basics such as socialization and litter training. Once you've got these down pat, you can begin expanding your repertoire and adding tricks up their furry sleeves!

Socializing Your New Kitten

Getting a Tuxedo kitten from a reputable breeder means that your kitten is already on the way to proper socialization skills. But if your kitten still seems a bit skittish and shy rather than the friendly and affectionate cat that Tuxedo cats are known for, then it is up to you to supplement their socialization - and this must be done as soon as possible!

The ages from before 4 to 14 weeks of age are crucial to a kitten's proper socialization. This is important because he might never outgrow the natural caution and suspiciousness that most kittens have at a very young age. If they still retain these characteristics until they grow mature, you will have a very stressed-out cat that hides at the sight and sound of every strange new thing. Another disadvantage of improper socialization is that the kitten might grow up naturally averse to you or the rest of your family, and while she is part of your household, you might never experience the kind of loving loyalty and affection which Tuxedos naturally have.

Socializing a kitten is not very complicated. Just keep in mind that you shouldn't push the kitten too much too soon - especially when he is still partly dependent on her mother and the rest of his siblings.

Start out with small doses of daily and gentle handling at about 4 weeks. Once the kitten gets used to you and to being handled by humans, you can slowly begin to start expanding his range of experiences. All these should be done in a positive atmosphere, however, since the lesson you are aiming to teach him is self-confidence in the face of new and strange experiences. For instance:

- Expose him to short bursts of gentle human handling by different people
- Begin exposing him to different sights, sounds and smells around the house
- Early grooming, which is recommended to build the habit of a cat that is used to regular grooming sessions, is also a good way to socialize your kitten and to get her used to human handling.
- Consider getting her used to the feel of a collar, and then later on, a leash. While you might not need to do this for all cats, you might find this learned behavior coming in handy later on for your Tuxedo. The Tuxedo is a large breed, and being a large breed, they can be prone to obesity. Eventually, you might find it necessary to take your cat out for a walk. Besides which, taking your little kitten out for short distance walks - even if it is only until the yard - is a good learning experience that will also expand his range of experiences. As your cat grows, you can also begin experimenting with the use of a harness.

- You can also provide him with a range of different cat toys which you can use to play with him and build your bond
- Take him with you out of the house, whether it is only for short walks, for a car ride, or a visit to the vet. During all these experiences, you should always be present and reassuring to your cat, as they will seek some form of security from you - especially if they are only just beginning to be weaned from their mother.

Once you have begun to properly socialize your kitten, it should continue throughout the rest of the cat's life. There will always be new experiences waiting for your Tuxedo, and new avenues to explore. Proper socialization can also be the beginning of a wide variety of additional training for your Tuxedo.

Litter Training for Kittens

If all goes well during the kitten's formative years, you will likely not have to do any litter training at all. In general, the elimination habits of cats are standard: they dig, eliminate, and then cover. This is instinctive, and comes from a need to hide the smell of their waste from predators.

Part of good litter habits is also your responsibility half the time, however. Make sure that it is located in a place where there is at least a modicum of privacy and where he will not be disturbed, which is also within easy reach. And keep the litter box clean - scooping twice a day and topping it off with additional litter granules, and cleaning and scrubbing the litter box at least once a week. Many times, behavioral problems regarding cats that suddenly refuse to use their litter box can be traced to their natural fastidiousness. Much as humans are averse to using a dirty toilet, neither will your cat be all that fond of using a dirty litter box. Other possible reasons for a behavioral problem among cats who refuse to use the litter box is a box that is of the right size, the wrong depth, or multiple users (i.e., different cats using the same box). Their sudden refusal to use the litter box may sometimes be due to the strong odor of cleaning chemicals you are using. Sometimes a cat may prefer using two separate boxes - one for urinating, and another for defecating; or he may prefer a specific brand of litter. As you get to know your Tuxedo, you'll figure out the quirks of his personality, including his elimination habits, and you can adjust accordingly.

Clicker Training for Teaching Tuxedo Cats Tricks

Yes, these gentle giants are intelligent and willing enough to be taught a trick or two. Some trainers who recommend using the clicker training method have reported great success in teaching Tuxedos tricks such as shaking hands, high five's, and even fetching!

No matter which trick you decide to teach your cat first, the training basics are the same. By associating the sound of a clicker with desired behavior and a treat, your Tuxedo has the capacity to pick up a variety of tricks in no time!

Here is a basic guideline to using the clicker training method to training your Tuxedo:

- First of all, get a clicker. You can purchase this at your local pet store, or online. This is a small, handheld device that makes a clicking sound when a button is pressed.

- You can use a flashlight to indicate targeted behavior. For instance, if you want them to get on top of a chair, use the light to point out the chair to let him know what your desired behavior is.

- Finally, the last factor in this training is some pre-selected treats that you can give as rewards. Make sure this is something he likes and which he will eat quickly and easily. The focus is, after all, the training, and not the food. Eventually, you will eliminate the food altogether and use only the clicker, so you need to be able to move easily past the treats to continuous training.

Simply put, the clicker training method integrates these three elements noted above: the light to indicate desired behavior, a clicker that should be sounded at the same time that the desired behavior is being performed, and the treat that follows afterwards.

Using the clicker simultaneously with the desired behavior helps them identify which behavior is being rewarded later on. Done consistently and over time, they will gradually associate the clicker with positive and desired behavior.

You might begin by first introducing your Tuxedo to the clicker itself so that it does not get spooked later on. Have them come near the clicker, allow them to sniff it, and as you click, give them a reward. This begins their associating the clicker with something positive. As much as possible, the clicker should only be used during training, and should always be associated with rewards. This teaches them that the clicker is a good thing. Eventually, the association is formed that the behavior you are clicking is also a good thing.

Over time, you can expand the number and variety of tricks you can teach your Tuxedo. The intelligence and natural devotion of this breed makes them easy learners. Just make sure to keep training sessions short, and always a positive experience. This is a wonderful way to nurture the bond between you and your cat, while also giving them mental and physical stimulation at the same time.

Chapter Seven: Grooming Your Tuxedo Cat

One of the reasons for the Tuxedo's great popularity is that it is relatively low maintenance in terms of grooming. Cats are fussy and fastidious by nature, so you will not have a lot of work to do. But because the Tuxedo does have a very long and elegant coat, some regular grooming is required. At least a weekly brushing session should suffice to keep their coats free of mats. But if you are showing, then you will have to learn how to bathe your Tuxedo! But this is also true for any Tuxedo owner - while you may not have to bathe your cat regularly, sometimes you might need to, especially when the abundant fur along the tail area gets a little dirty with their poo.

Tips for Grooming Tuxedo Cats

While a weekly coat care grooming session might be sufficient, you might want to get into the habit of daily or regular brushing with a soft bristle cat brush. These come with two sides, which you can alternatively use to brush and comb. You might want to focus on the Tuxedo's tail, hind quarters, and behind the ears, and brushing these regularly can keep mats from developing in the first place.

That said, sometimes matting cannot be avoided, and to be able to help the Tuxedo maintain his beautiful coat, at least a weekly coat care grooming session is recommended to winnow out any matting or tangles that may have formed despite your best efforts. You will need the following:

- de-matting comb
- grooming rake

- metal comb
- clippers
- eye wipes
- cotton balls to clean the ears

Start out by working out any tangles or knots in the coat using a metal comb. Be sure to start near the end instead of near the skin, holding the fur near the skin to lessen painful tugging. Go slow and a little at a time, carefully separating the tangled fur. As an alternative, you can use a fine-tooth comb like a flea comb for really tight knots.

Next, you can use the grooming rake to remove any dead undercoat. Remember that the Tuxedo's coat has two layers, one of which is the fluffier and softer undercoat. If ignored, this can certainly mat. Gently running the grooming rake along the fur will enable you to remove most of the dead undercoat. You'll probably be surprised at the amount of hair you'll get! Just continue gently stripping those out - then you'll discover just why your Tuxedo does need your help in maintaining all that abundant fur!

If you do find mats that are just too far gone, trying to brush them out will only hurt your cat, and eventually they might dislike grooming sessions altogether. Using a flea comb, position this between the skin and the mat, and then snip alongside the comb near the matted fur side.

Finish it off with eye wipes to clean their eyes and nose area, or you can just use a warm, damp facecloth for the face. Finish it off with cotton balls damped with warm water to clean the inside of the ears, going slowly so as not to damage the sensitive portion of their inner ears.

Tips for Bathing Tuxedo Cats

Yes, cats do need the occasional bath. You might want to start them out while they are kittens, so that even though they will probably never get to really like a bath, they will at least be trained to tolerate it. Bathing also needs to be done in a positive atmosphere, and should your cat wish to escape, just let him. Make it as painless as possible so that he does not learn to view bath time as something to be avoided at all costs. For the more mature Tuxedos, you might want to finish trimming their claws before bathing them.

Remember that the Tuxedo's abundant fur is designed to keep them warm during winter and the rainy season, so it will not get wet easily. You might want to use water in a sufficient-sized tub, or in the kitchen sink, depending on your cat's size. Keep this at a nice temperature, and just put your cat in and get him wet. Use quality cat shampoo and start rubbing it in. Add water as needed to really get the fur wet. Try to make the shampooing as quick, efficient, and as painless as possible.

Rinse well, and be sure to get all the soap off, because he'll be washing himself afterwards, and you don't want him ingesting any soap that you might not have rinsed off. Use towels to dry him off, and he's good to go. Using a dryer is probably not a good idea since this might scare him. You might want to pick a warm or hot day to give him a bath so that he can dry himself off in the sun.

Needless to say, each cat is different and unique, and you will probably need to adjust your methods depending on his preferences. It is always a good idea to start the habit of bathing and grooming when he is still a kitten though, keeping to it regularly and consistently so that it becomes a habit that stays with him throughout his life.

Other Grooming Tasks

There are other grooming tasks in addition to regular brushing and bathing, and this includes clipping your cat's claws and brushing his teeth. This sort of rounds out the grooming tasks for a Tuxedo cat, to keep this gentle giant looking spiffy and sharp!

Brushing Your Cat's Teeth

Yes, occasionally a good session of tooth brushing is good for your Tuxedo! this helps prevent tooth decay and dental infections. Look for quality cat toothbrush and cat toothpaste, and while regular brushing is ideal, doing so about two or three times a week is a good routine.

Clipping Your Cat's Claws

Clipping your cat's claws is a more humane option to de-clawing them. While providing them with a good scratching post will keep their nails reasonably sharp and trimmed, occasionally you might want to trim them once in a while. Invest in some quality cat nail clippers. Using them should be pretty easy.

Just squeeze the paw until the claw is revealed. Press them all the way out, and clip. Be cautious when clipping so that you don't cut the quick, or the flesh beneath the nail. Clip conservatively, especially if it is your first time. Without enough practice, claw clipping should be a quick and straightforward routine, and is actually one of the easiest parts of Tuxedo grooming.

Chapter Eight: Breeding Your Tuxedo Cat

Anyone who undertakes to breed Tuxedo cats should first be aware of the huge responsibility this entails. Yes, Tuxedos are a very lovable breed, and pedigreed Tuxedos do cost good money, so it is understandable that some people might consider it desirable to try for a litter of kittens. But a prospective breeder should know that breeding cats can consume much of their time, energy, and money, so if you are only looking to make some extra money, this may not prove to be a worthwhile venture for you.

On the other hand, you should be fully committed to promoting the best interests of the breed, which means that you have to be thorough, selective, and well-informed before you even try to breed your cats. You will be responsible for the health and wellbeing of both the queen and her kittens, up until the time when you are able to place the kittens with good homes, so this is not something for the casual or spontaneous breeder to venture into.

There are those who recommend that anybody who wants to be a breeder should always start first by showing cats. This is a good way to learn about the breed, the breed standard for Tuxedos, and to network with other cat enthusiasts and cat breeders. A good and dedicated acquaintanceship to cat showing should ground any prospective breeder with realistic expectations and actual experience in dealing with the Tuxedo cats, and what it really means to breed responsibly.

That said, when done right, breeding your Tuxedo can be a very satisfying and fulfilling experience. This chapter contains some basic information, tips and guidelines that will be useful for any prospective cat breeder. First we will begin with some basic cat breeding information, and later we will take a look at some practical tips for caring for your new kittens.

Basic Cat Breeding Information

The assumption here is that you have selected a good queen and stud for breeding, and the requisite health checks have been conducted. There should be ample space for your cattery, and you should be prepared to devote a lot of time, effort and energy into seeing that the breeding process, up to the time of pregnancy, labor and weaning the kittens - goes well. It is also a good idea to have a good savings set aside for necessary expenses such as cat food, a litter and a kitten pen, and some unforeseen costs as well - such as veterinary services just in case you run into any problems.

The Queen

A good queen should be healthy and fit, and psychologically well-adjusted for motherhood. Most recommend that a cat should not be mated before her first or second year, and during this time you should already be looking into prospective studs. Be aware that cats are quite prolific, and there could be many instances of unplanned or accidental pregnancies if the owner is not careful. Female cats can mate multiple times when they are in heat, so it is not an uncommon occurrence that a litter may have been sired by more than one father. Be watchful of your queen when she is in heat - don't allow her to escape unless you wish her to mate with many of the local toms who will surely be hanging around outside! It is probably a good rule of thumb to be particularly watchful and protective of a breeding queen. When allowed to mate naturally, it is estimated that a cat can have a full litter at least three times a year!

On the other hand, it is not recommended to let a cat "call" three times in succession without mating. Since they are induced ovulators, they will only release their mature female eggs after they are mated. If a cat is unable to mate for long, there is an increased chance that cysts might form in her ovaries. If a queen is not allowed to mate for too many cycles, the eggs will accumulate until the next estrus. This can lead to two potential problems: a cat that ends up carrying too large a litter, or older eggs being carried over from previous cycles, which can result in congenitally defective kittens.

If your cat is calling and you do not want her to mate, you should ask your veterinarian about the possible ways of managing her heat cycle and fertility. This is generally done through three ways: the use of hormones, mechanical stimulation, or with the service of a vasectomized male. Consult with your veterinarian regarding these three ways of managing a queen's fertility.

A cat can have her first heat at the age of six months, and they are seasonally polyestrous. This means that they will come into heat during certain seasons of the year - usually in the spring and summer, though cats who are kept indoors may cycle year-round. Another interesting thing to note about the cat's heat cycle is that they are reflex or induced ovulators. This means that they need to be bred first before they will ovulate. This would explain why cats in heat will mate multiple times, and why there will still be signs of heat several days after mating. This can lead to what is known as super fecundity, or when the queen's litter has been fathered by more than one male. Sometimes, a surge of hormones early during pregnancy can result in mixed gestational stages of the kittens inside her uterus, who will then be in different stages of development.

Perhaps the first thing any potential cat breeder should learn is how to manage a breeding queen - especially during times of heat and she is calling. If you are not planning on breeding, unless you wish to end up with litters of kittens during your cat's lifetime, the responsible thing for you to do is to have your female cat spayed. Not only does this eliminate the chances of unplanned pregnancies, but doing so before she reaches her first heat cycle will reduce her risk of mammary cancer.

The Feline Heat Cycle

You will recognize when your queen is in heat. During the first two days, or proestrus, she will be "calling." Some behavioral signs of this are rubbing, excessive friendliness, yowling, rolling, and a frequent desire to escape. During this time, she will also exhibit a unique posture of standing arched with her tail straight up, with her back and rear legs stiffening whenever they are touched. She will not allow mating during this time, however, and she will usually fold her tail between her hind legs to prevent this.

The second stage, or Estrus, is when mating occurs. This can last for up to ten days, though if coitus happens earlier, it can end after about three to four days. Copulation releases a luteinizing hormone (LH) that stimulates ovulation, though the levels can vary with different queens. For some, it may take several mating sessions before ovulation can be induced. After a successful breeding, estrus terminates and diestrus begins.

It is recommended that you leave the tom and the queen alone together for several days during the estrus stage. This will allow multiple mating session, and ensures a successful pregnancy. Some breeders recommend providing the tom room to escape after breeding, because the queen can get aggressive immediately after mating. She will also groom herself frantically, and she will not allow anyone near her for about an hour afterwards. After this, she becomes receptive again, and mating can resume. Again, she may allow multiple males to mate with her, so it is a good idea to keep her relatively isolated during this time, where the selected stud is the only male with access to her.

If the breeding was not successful, the queen will enter an interfollicular stage known as interestrus. This may last for about a week, during which there is no reproductive activity. Then she enters a new cycle of proestrus and estrus. If, on the other hand, she was mated and ovulated, but did not become pregnant, she enters a stage known as metestrus that can last for some 5-7 weeks. Again, there will be no reproductive activity during this time. After this stage, she will again enter a new heat cycle of proestrus and estrus.

If the mating was successful, however, the gestation period will last for about 59-65 days, or about 9-10 weeks. If, for any reason, she loses her kittens, she will again enter the estrus stage after 2-3 weeks. If she successfully carried her litter until birth, a new heat cycle will begin again when the kittens are about 8-10 weeks old.

Pregnancy

Pregnancy can be confirmed at around 3 to 4 weeks. Her nipples will become more pink and prominent, and the telltale baby bump will start to show at around 4 weeks. Queens with small litters will take even longer to "show" than those with a larger litter. To date, this is the only safe method of recognizing feline pregnancy.

The nutritional need of your queen will increase during pregnancy, and their appetite should begin to increase at around the fifth or sixth week of pregnancy. It is recommended that you begin to increase their diet by about twenty-five percent, making sure that they have a nourishing and well-balanced diet. It is a good idea to speak with your veterinarian so that you can plan out the dietary changes that will be suitable for your cat during her pregnancy.

You should also begin preparing for her due date. You might notice her seeking out secluded areas, spending more time with you and less with others in the family, or a marked hostility towards strangers. Prepare a birthing area such as a delivery box with sufficient room, and a second box in which she could move the kittens after she has given birth. Keep this in a relatively secluded area of the home where she can have peace and quiet, and try to get her used to this area some time before her actual due date. You can also begin to put together a birthing kit in expectation of the due date, which would include items such as towels, a clean bowl, sterile gloves, blunt-end scissors, betadine, pediatric bulb syringes, a tube feeder, and dental floss or suture to tie the umbilical cords if necessary. Be sure to have the number of the nearest emergency vet clinic on hand, some pen and paper, and a clock nearby.

In general, many cats are able to give birth without much trouble, but you should always be at hand, ready to lend a hand when needed. If this is your first time to assist during cat labor, you should probably seek out a mentor to stay with you and guide you during the process. Cat labor can be a frightening and stressful experience for first-timers, so while you can read up on the subject prior to the date, a friendly and helping hand with practical experience is always good to have alongside you during this time. Being able to act efficiently when needed can mean the difference between losing or saving a kitten.

Chapter Nine: Showing Your Tuxedo Cat

If you are considering showing your Tuxedo Cat, then it is as well to get acquainted with this breed's rich history as a show cat. This chapter will also give you an overview of the Breed Standards in several different associations, and some practical hints and tips that will guide you as you prepare for cultivating a magnificent cat that just seems naturally meant to shine.

Tuxedo Cat Breed Standards

The Tuxedo Cat is truly a universally popular feline, beloved by many people all over the world. In 1968, the Tuxedo Breeders and Fanciers Association (MCBFA), an international breed association for the Tuxedo Cat was founded. The breed is also recognized by a number of different cat organizations all over the world. These would include the following:

- American Cat Association (ACA)
- American Cat Fanciers Association (ACFA)
- Canadian Cat Association (CCA)
- Cat Fanciers' Association (CFA)
- Cat Fanciers' Federation (CFF)
- Fédération Internationale Féline (FIFe)
- Governing Council of the Cat Fancy (GCCF)
- The International Cat Association (TICA)

Necessarily, the Breed Standards for the Tuxedo Cat varies depending on which organization is hosting the show, so you will have to pay particular attention to the published standards, depending on which organization or association you are registered with. There are slight variations in standards, though of course the differences are not very great.

Below, and as a sort of general guideline, we will first take a look at the MCBFA's published Breed Standard, and then later take a look at some of the noticeable variations in the Breed Standards of the different organizations listed above.

1.   The Tuxedo Breeders and Fancier's Association's (MCBFA) Tuxedo Cat Breed Standard

General

The Tuxedo Cat is solid and rugged, with a slow maturation. Females are somewhat smaller than the males.

Head

The head is medium in length and width, and there is a squareness to the muzzle. Some broadening is allowable in males. The cheekbones are high; the nose is medium with no break or bump. The chin is firm and in line with the upper lip and nose.

The ears are large, wide at the base, moderately pointed, and well-tufted. Lynx-like tipping is considered desirable.

Body and Neck

The body is medium to large, muscular and broad-chested. It is also long, with proportional parts, creating a rectangular appearance. There is a definite squareness to the rump, and the neck is medium in length.

Legs and Paws

The legs are wide set, substantial, and medium in length. The paws are also large, round, and well-tufted. There should be five toes in front, and four toes in back.

Tail

The tail should be long, equal in length to the body (or the distance from the end of the rump to the shoulders), wide at the base and tapering. The fur should be full, long, and flowing.

2.   The International Cat Association (TICA) Tuxedo Cat Breed Standard

General

This is a large breed with big ears, a broad chest, substantial bone structure, and a long, hard-muscled and rectangular body, with a long, flowing tail, and tufted large feet. Overall balance and proportion are considered essential, no single feature dominating over others.

Head, Eyes, and Ears

The head is broad and shaped like a modified wedge. It should be proportional to the body, and slightly longer than it is wide. A distinct muzzle break can be seen under high and prominent cheekbones. The chin is firm, in line with the upper lip, and wide and deep to complete the square muzzle.

The eyes are large, slightly oval, with the outer corner pointing towards the base of the ear. The eyes can be of any shade of green and/or gold, though blue and odd-eyes are accepted among whites and particolors.

The ears are large, wide at the base, the outer base set just above the level of the top of the eye. The ears are set fairly high, and the inner edge of the bases of both ears not more than an ear's width apart. It is taller than its width, moderately pointed, which appears taller due to lynx tips.

Body, Legs, Feet and Tail

The bones and musculature are substantial, with a large and long torso, broad chest, and level back. The legs are medium in length, and the feet are large, round, and well-tufted.

Additional toes are allowable on the fore or hind paws, though there should only be a maximum of 7 toes on any one foot. Symmetrical expression is preferred.

The tail should be at least as long as the body, wide at the base, and tapering to the tip, with full, flowing fur.

The temperament must be unchallenging. Though it may exhibit fear, seek to flee, or complain loudly, it should not threaten to harm.

Allowances

Allowances are given for size differences between males and females. A tight ear set is also allowed in kittens, and a wider ear set in mature adults. Polydactyly, which may express itself in an extra dew claw or extra toes, is acceptable.

Penalties

The following traits are penalized:

- Slanted or almond-shaped eyes

- Very close ears, or those that are set straight up. Narrow bases, wide set, or flared ears are also penalized
- Weak or receding, or narrow chin
- Prominent whisker pads on the muzzle
- A Roman nose, straight, or with a pronounced bump
- Narrow torso
- Short tail
- Any of the toes or dewclaws not touching the table
- Lack of the slight undercoat or belly shag. An overall even coat is also penalized
- Signs of definite challenge or threat to harm in the temperament

Disqualifications

The following, on the other hand, automatically disqualify:

- A cat that bites
- Evidence of an intent to deceive
- Adult male cats without two descended testicles
- Missing tail, either in whole or in part, except as authorized
- More than five toes one each front foot, or four toes on each back foot, unless proven as a result of injury
- Crossed eyes
- Markedly smaller size, not in keeping with the breed

Chapter Ten: Keeping Your Tuxedo Cat Healthy

Tuxedo Cats are generally healthy, hardy and robust. The breed has adapted itself to the harsh New England climate, and they are good hunters, so this breed is a survivor. That said, there are some health concerns that are of particular concern in Tuxedos. While most responsible breeders do their best to screen out potential diseases by breeding only healthy cats, there is never any guarantee that a cat will not get some disease during his lifetime. The best thing that you, as the owner, can do, is to be aware of which particular health conditions Tuxedo cats are prone to, what the symptoms are, and the treatment options. Virtually any disease that is caught and treated early is less worrisome than one that has gone undetected for a long time.

Common Health Problems Affecting Tuxedo Cats

Some of the common conditions that may affect Tuxedo Cats include:

- Feline Hypertrophic Cardiomyopathy (HCM)
- Spinal Muscular Atrophy (SMA)
- Hip Dysplasia (HD)
- Polycystic Kidney Disease (PKD)

Feline Hypertrophic Cardiomyopathy

Feline Hypertrophic Cardiomyopathy (HCM) is the most common heart disease in cats, and it is potentially fatal. It is the number one cause of spontaneous death among indoor adult cats. This is a genetic or inherited condition, and is estimated to show up in 1 out of 3 among the Tuxedo cat population.

In HCM, there is a thickening in the heart's left chamber, which restricts blood flow and causes the heart to overwork. This used to be a genuine problem to screen out because most of the time, the first and only symptom among cats is sudden death to HCM. And because it doesn't manifest until a cat is a young adult or older, breeding out this condition was not easy. By the time it manifests, a cat may already have sired several litters - general good health notwithstanding.

The good news is that the genetic carrier for this disease has already been identified. A Dr. Kathryn Meurs has isolated the genetic mutation which causes HCM this disease. DNA-based screening is now available to identify cats that are carriers, and this will be significant in the breeding of cats, thus reducing the risk of this genetic condition being passed on to new generations.

But this is a relatively recent development, and given that this is a congenital condition that does seem to occur among Tuxedos, knowing when to recognize the symptoms is always a good idea.

HCM is not an easy condition to detect outside of DNA screening - but if you find your cat manifesting respiratory difficulties, sudden hind leg paralysis due to clotting, loss of appetite, lethargy, coughing, severe weight loss, a weak pulse, abnormal heart murmurs, a bluish discoloration in the footpads and nailbeds, or a sudden collapse, you had better bring your Tuxedo to a vet. After ruling out other possible causes such as hyperthyroidism, hypertension, and cardiac arrhythmias, HCM can be diagnosed through a non-invasive ultrasound called an echocardiogram, supported by x-rays, an EKG, and an electrocardiogram.

There is currently no cure for HCM. The treatment options for Tuxedos diagnosed with HCM are mostly medications that aim to relieve the symptoms - such as by controlling heart rate, alleviating pulmonary congestion, and reducing the likelihood of thromboembolism. When feasible, a catheter can be used to remove the pleural fluid to help the cat breathe more easily.

The prognosis is variable - HCM is a progressive disease, which means that it will grow worse over time, though the rate of progression is also variable. Depending on the cat's response to medication and treatment, some can still have an excellent quality of life for several years.

Spinal Muscular Atrophy (SMA)

SMA is a non-fatal, genetic condition that is well-documented among Tuxedos. In SMA, the neurons in the spinal cord that activate skeletal muscles in the trunk and limbs are compromised, which leads to muscle weakness and degeneration. Possible symptoms include a swaying rear end, abnormal posture, difficulty in jumping, or an awkward landing when they jump down. If you feel at their hind legs, you may be able to recognize reduced muscle mass.

Symptoms can manifest as early as 3-4 months, and while not fatal, SMA can cause weakened muscle development. SMA does not affect the cat's appetite or their capacity in excretion. Thankfully, neither are the symptoms fatal, and aside from weakened muscles, a cat can otherwise live a normal life. To date, the oldest diagnosed cats are in their 8-9 years of age. On the other hand, however, some cats diagnosed with SMA may end up with paralysis in the hind legs.

A DNA test is available to diagnose and/or screen carriers of this genetic condition. Take note that this is an autosomal recessive trait, which means that two copies of the gene, or both parents who are carriers, are required for their offspring to develop SMA. There is no treatment for SMA, but some cats do seem to stabilize and may still live comfortably for many years.

Hip Dysplasia

Hip Dysplasia is an inherited trait that Tuxedos are prone to. In the same way that this is more prevalent among the larger breed of dogs, hip dysplasia is also more common among large breed cats. A genetic predisposition for this condition is inherited, but the condition itself develops over time. There is a laxity in the hip joints which can be destabilized by having to bear abnormal weight. When this happens, the cartilage can disintegrate, resulting in arthritis and pain. As the cartilage disintegrates, the femoral head and acetabulum rub together with each step, and this may lead to osteoarthritis.

The symptoms depend on the severity, and while some cats may experience little or no pain, it may eventually cause severe lameness in others. If untreated, hip dysplasia can be crippling.

Some of the symptoms to watch out for are slow movement in the cat, a stiffness in walking, lameness, or a reluctance in running or jumping. If caught early, the condition can be managed, and some experts recommend weight management, massage, and exercise therapy. It is imperative that the cat should not be exposed to cold weather, since this might induce arthritis. Alternatively, medication or surgery can help relieve the pain for the more advanced cases.

This is another condition that can be tested for, and any cat breeder is responsible for having the hips of their Tuxedo breeding pair x-rayed and graded. This can be done when the cat is about two years of age, and a good breeder must have a result that is either fair, good, or excellent.

Polycystic Kidney Disease (PKD)

PKD is another inherited disorder; it is a slow and progressive disease affecting the kidneys. A kitten will usually be born with cysts, or fluid-filled cavities, in the kidneys. These will grow larger as the cat matures, and it is estimated that there could be anywhere from 20 to 200 cysts present.

The symptoms can manifest early, though sometimes not until 3 to 10 years of age. The initial signs are usually quite ambiguous - such as lack of appetite, depression, drinking and urinating more often, a less shiny coat. As the condition progresses, the symptoms can also be more severe, including blood in the urine, bad breath, vomiting, and weight loss. Eventually, this might lead to incurable kidney failure. It bears stressing, however, that the symptoms are very variable, and some cats with PKD may not display any of the symptoms at all - though these are usually those with very little or small cysts.

As with most inherited conditions, the best way is to remove cats diagnosed with PKD from breeding programs. This minimizes the risk of transmission to offspring. A DNA test is available to screen for the responsible gene, but at present, this test is only available for Persians and Exotics. Diagnosis is usually done by ultrasound. Tuxedos that have been diagnosed with PKD should not be bred, and cats that are intended for breeding should be tested at a year old, and retested again at the age of 2.

While there is no cure, treatment options are geared towards managing the symptoms. In cases of dehydration or vomiting, for instance, intravenous feeding for several days, followed by a special diet, is prescribed. Alternatively, therapy, a special low protein diet, and medication may be recommended to help alleviate some of the symptoms.

Preventing Illness with Vaccinations

Over the years, vaccines have been developed against potentially lethal diseases. Essentially, vaccines contain a minute, weakened or killed dose of the disease itself, in order to stimulate the production of antibodies within the cat's system. The memory of these antibodies is retained, and anytime there is re-exposure to the same pathogen, the body immediately produces more of the same antibodies. That is why vaccines are named for the diseases that they target - and in this way, immunity is built up within the cat's body against many of the lethal feline diseases.

Some vaccines are necessary and legally required - these are considered "core" vaccines, and are obligatory. The core vaccines include those for feline rhinotrcheitis, calicivirus, paleukepenia, and rabies. Rabies vaccines are required to be renewed once every one to three years, depending on your local laws.

On the other hand, "non-core" vaccines, while not mandatory, are administered depending on whether it is needed. Your veterinarian can give you the best advice on whether any of the following vaccines are needed, depending on the state of feline health in your area or region: Pneumonitis, FeLV or Feline Leukemia, FIV or more commonly known as Feline AIDS, FIP or Feline Infectious Peritonitis, Chlamydia felis,

Bordetella, and Giardia. If your Vet recommends any of these non-core vaccines, be sure to discuss with him the reason why they are needed.

Proper information and informed decisions about the administration of non-core vaccines are becoming a source of debate in the veterinary world. It seems that too much vaccinations may actually have the opposite effect of giving your pet immunity against certain diseases. The administration of a second dose of the same vaccine, when the antibodies produced with the first vaccine are still in the bloodstream, might just end up deactivating those antibodies, thus exposing your pet to unnecessary risk. That aside from certain adverse reactions that a cat may have from being vaccinated too often. Then again, others argue that any adverse reactions are rare, and that it is still safer for your pet to receive the recommended vaccines, including the annual booster shots.

Regardless of which side of the debate you come down on, however, it is important that your cat be in good health at the time of vaccination. You will be introducing foreign agents in your cat's system, and he needs to be in good condition in order to produce the necessary antibodies. If you suspect that your cat is having an adverse reaction to a vaccine, bring him to a Vet immediately.

Below is a sample schedule of feline vaccinations, though please remember that each cat's vaccine schedule will have to depend on different and variable factors such as age, environment, lifestyle, and the cat's medical history.

Chapter Eleven: Daily Care for a Tuxedo Cat

One of the most important things you can do for your Tuxedo cat on a daily basis is to interact. This is a very loving and extremely loyal breed. Tuxedos want to be with their humans, thriving on attention, affection, and play.

Of course, you must meet your cat's physical needs, but you have a responsibility to address the emotional requirements of your Tuxedo as well. Cats, especially Tuxedo cats, are not the detached loners they are made out to be.

A Tuxedo cat is a people cat. The first thing he wants and needs is you.

After that? Some nice service at the food bowl would be much appreciated for starters.

Nutrition Food and Water

All cats, regardless of their breed are carnivores. A dog can be fed a vegetarian diet and do just fine, but cats have a high need for protein.

Most breeders are in agreement that Tuxedos do best on a mixed diet of dry and wet food. Some catteries advocate feeding a "raw" diet, while others use high-quality commercial canned foods.

Some types of cats should not be allowed to free feed (have access to food left in the bowl throughout the day), but this is not the case with the Tuxedo cat.

It's perfectly acceptable to leave kibble out for your cat, especially in the first three years of life. Remember that your Tuxedo will not reach full maturity until age five, at which time it's best to cut back a little on the dry food to avoid weight gain.

Selecting a High-Quality Food

Discuss the matter of food selection with both your breeder and your vet. Always go with the highest quality food you can afford.

The general rule of thumb with commercial pet foods is the cheaper the price, the greater the amount of plant fillers the food will contain.

Cats need twice as much protein per pound as humans, and they need fats. They don't need plant-based carbohydrates.

The Raw Diet

{Note: The following is provided for informational purposes only and does not constitute an endorsement of the raw diet. Because the raw diet is used by many reputable Tuxedo breeders, the material is being offered in the interest of a complete, well-rounded consideration of daily Tuxedo care. Always discuss feeding programs with both your breeder and your vet before dramatically altering your cat's diet}

The raw diet for both dogs and cats remains controversial. Many veterinarians are strictly against the practice, but those who are interested in holistic health care approaches are beginning to see merit in this eating program.

The theory behind this method of feeding is to give the animal the kind of raw foodstuffs it would eat if it were living in its wild, natural state. For an obligate carnivore like a cat, the raw diet consists of anything that could be obtained from a whole, fresh carcass.

Veterinarian Concerns with the Raw Diet

The potential danger of a cat contracting salmonella poisoning from raw food is an often cited as a concern by veterinary professionals.

While it is true that felines can get salmonella, it's important to remember that because their intestinal tract is short, cats have strong bacteria in their stomachs that allow them to digest foods we would never be able to eat.

With meticulous handling of the food itself, thorough hand washing, and the purchase of fresh products (mainly fresh poultry well within its expiration date) salmonella should not be an issue.

The best rule of thumb is to never feed your cat anything you wouldn't eat yourself. (That being said there are many human foods that are toxic to cats, a subject we will touch on shortly.)

Vets also express concern about nutritional balance, pointing out, quite rightly, that commercial cat foods have known and regulated amounts of specific vitamins and minerals.

If you do decide to feed your Tuxedo a raw diet, it is imperative that you understand what nutrients your pet requires and take the necessary steps to make sure they are met.

Important Considerations with Raw Food

- Serve only raw chicken and beef, never pork or fish.
- Never keep raw food in the refrigerator past 2-3 days.
- Do not microwave raw cat food. Let it to sit out for a short period until it reaches room temperature.

- Keep your preparation space and all implements and receptacles scrupulously clean.
- Purchase a good quality grinder capable of adequately handling small bones.

Do Your Research Before Changing Your Cat's Diet

Before you consider putting any domestic animal on a raw diet, research the topic fully. Because cats are carnivores, there is a degree of logic to feeding them what they would be eating if they were hunting and killing their own prey.

However -- and this is an important "however" -- an incorrectly prepared raw diet can be deadly for your pet. The raw principle includes feeding bones. This represents both a choking hazard and the potential for throat and stomach tears and punctures from splinters.

It cannot be stressed strongly enough that a raw diet must be prepared according to set recipes with the use of special equipment to safeguard the health of your cat.

Things to NEVER Feed Your Tuxedo cat

Cats are just as susceptible to developing poor eating habits as their humans. They can get a "sweet" tooth, and they can be highly skilled panhandlers. Don't let this business get started!

Feeding your cat "people" food not only contributes to weight gain and an unhealthy diet, but it also raises the real danger of your inadvertently giving your beloved pet something that is harmless to you, but toxic to him.

- Never give a cat any form of caffeine including coffee, and do not let him eat chocolate.

The real culprits in these food items are the methylxanthines found in cacao seeds. The extract is used in chocolate, and in a variety of beverages including soda.

If your cat eats any of these items, a series of dangerous reactions can result. These may include: vomiting, diarrhea, excessive thirst, panting, irregular heart rate, seizures, tremors, and even death.

Other foods that contain some level of toxicity for cats include, but are not limited to: alcohol, avocado, grapes, raisins, yeast dough, eggs, onions, garlics, and chives.

Do not let the cat get into anything that contains the sweetener xylitol, which can lead to liver failure among other complications, and do not let the animal eat an excess of salty treats. This can create an increased danger of fatal dehydration.

While it is certainly true that your Tuxedo cat may enjoy a dish of milk or cream, proceed with caution. Cats don't produce enough lactase (an enzyme) to break down milk in their digestive system, a deficiency responsible for diarrhea and uncomfortable gastrointestinal upset.

Many adult cats are actually lactose intolerant, and experience the same level of discomfort from the condition seen in humans.

Adult Tuxedo cats don't need milk, and they don't get any real nutritional benefit from consuming it. If your cat shows signs of stomach upset after drinking milk, don't feel as if you're taking away some beloved treat by not repeating the experiment.

"Treats" of any kind should make up less than 10% of your cat's diet anyway, and you certainly don't want to give him something that will just cause a tummy ache or worse.

Water is an Essential Component of Nutrition

Provide clean, fresh water for your cat at all times, and change the bowl often. Cats won't drink from a dirty water bowl, and many prefer to drink moving water.

Consider the option of purchasing a water bowl with a re-circulating fountain. This will not only keep the water cleaner, but it will attract the cat's interest and encourage him to drink more.

Feline water fountains are not terribly expensive, retailing for roughly $30 (£23). Do be forewarned that Tuxedos are attracted by motion of any kind and may play in their water a bit. Having to mop up a few splashes is a small price to pay, however, for ensuring that your cat stays well hydrated.

Estimating Food Costs is Difficult

Obviously, given all the variables and all the options for attending to your Tuxedo cat's nutritional needs, prices can vary widely — especially if you opt to feed your cat a raw diet; then you will be purchasing and preparing beef and chicken.

As a preventive health measure, a well-rounded, high-quality diet is your pet's best defense against disease and the simple effects of aging.

The standard advice is to buy the highest quality food you can afford, in both wet and dry variations.

Plan on feeding your Tuxedo twice a day, morning and evening with some type of wet food, (about 5.5 ounces / 14.17 grams per serving), and free feeding kibble (.25 to .50 a cup U.S. /0.208 to 0.416 cup UK per serving) throughout the day.

Conservatively, expect to spend about $50 (£33) per month on wet food and $25 (£17) on dry.

Depending on the style you choose, both food and water bowls should cost $5-$10 / £3-£7 each.

Litter and Litter Boxes

After food and water, one of your greatest responsibilities to your kitty is to provide a suitable and clean place to do the "business." Cats are fastidiously clean animals. If they go "off" their box, it's almost always for one of two reasons:

- They have an undiagnosed medical issue like a bladder infection and are experiencing pain getting in the box, which they are seeking to avoid by going somewhere else.
- They don't like the condition of their box and are looking for a more suitable place to eliminate.
- Cats are not all that fond of change anyway, and changes to their litter box environment can lead to disaster.

Litter Texture Matters to a Cat

When you bring your new Tuxedo kitten home, use whatever litter arrangement the baby has been used to at the cattery. Moving forward, your basic choices involve litter texture and box type.

Litters are available in:

- Traditional gravel or clay.

This is the least expensive option. As much as 10 lbs. (4.53 kg) can be purchased for around $2.50-$5.00 (£2-£4).

- Fine clumping sand. (Available in single and multi-cat formulations.)

Clumping litter is a good choice because many cats like the finer texture. (Be warned, if you have a vigorous digger, this stuff can fly.) NEVER flush clumping litter down the toilet unless the box specifically says the formulation is "flushable."

Many mainstream brands can be purchased in bulk. For instance: 42 lbs. (19 kg) $18 / £12

Designer brands that claim superior odor control with all natural ingredients are much more expensive, with as little as 1.4 lbs. (.63 kg) selling for $30 / £20

- Environmentally friendly plant based materials like pine.

These litters are also cost effective. For a pine litter, expect to pay about $10 / £7 for 20 lbs. (9.07 kg). Some cat owners report good success with these litters if the cat becomes accustomed to them early on, but older cats who are used to gravel or sand will likely balk when they find their box full of shavings.

- Absorbent crystals.

Crystals are a relatively new type of litter that claim to absorb and trap urine and inhibit bacterial growth. Most are made of amorphous silica gel and are biodegradable. For 8 lbs. (3.6 kg) you'll pay approximately $16 / £11

Cats do have definite litter preferences. If you are going to attempt to transition your cat to a new type of litter, offer two boxes: one with the old litter, and one with what they are already used to OR mix the two litter types, gradually phasing out the old litter.

If you just present your Tuxedo cat with a box full of something completely new, don't be surprised if you get a …. surprise.

Box Type is Also an Important Preference

- A simple, open litter pan or box is the tried and true standard. These units can be purchased for $6-$10 / £4-£6.

The major disadvantage with open pans is that litter scattering is a major problem, and many cats do not like to be "watched."

- Covered boxes hide the unsightly evidence, and afford kitty more privacy. Depending on size, you'll pay $30-$50 / £20-£33.
- Automatic self-scooping boxes are popular with humans for many reasons, but can send kitty running.

Expect to pay $150 to $200 (£98-£130) for a unit of this type, but leave the original box accessible until you're certain your cat will use the mechanical one.

Training and Playtime

Tuxedos love to interact with their humans, and as a breed, they are so highly observant, they catch on very quickly. They learn language well, and are quite aware when their humans are pleased with them.

Some experts say that all a cat requires is patience from their humans. Anyone who has tried to convince a feline to do anything might be tempted to say the patience flows in the other direction!

Tuxedos, however, have a boundless store of patience for the people they love, and so are highly agreeable to notions of training – and they're always up for a game!

Leash Training

While the Tuxedo is not one of the cat breeds that will take readily to being walked on a leash, they are highly intelligent and trainable cats. The most important aspect of leash training is having the correct equipment, principally a leash designed specifically for a cat.

These units, which resemble open vests, put the attachment for the lead at the back of the harness between the cat's shoulder blades, not at the throat.

A popular model, the Premier's Gentle Leader Come with Me Kitty Harness and Bungee Leash is priced at approximately $11 / £7. The included leash has a "springy" feel, which diminishes the sense of resistance a cat can feel – and object to – on a conventional lead.

A variation on this theme is a harness design with a broader mesh piece across the chest. An example of this design is the Coastal Pet Pink Mesh Cat Harness, which sells for $12 / £8.

Some cats like this style because it feels more secure against their bodies and doesn't return a binding sensation along the straps due to the wider design.

You will likely have to try both styles to find out which your Tuxedo prefers. At first, just get the cat used to wearing the harness around the house without the lead attached.

Don't make any fuss about putting the unit on. If kitty objects one day, stop and try again on the next. It's imperative that there be no negative associations in the cat's mind with any part of this process.

Some owners report good success just leaving the harness and leash lying around near the cat's bed or on the sofa so their cat can look it over and give it the feline sniff test.

If a cat is reluctant about wearing the harness at first, don't try to buckle it, just drape it over their shoulders. At first, the Tuxedo will walk right out of the whole silly business, but in time, he'll begin to let the harness hang there.

That will allow you to proceed to buckling it loosely in place, gradually tightening the straps or to an appropriate fit over time.

A good rule of thumb is that you want to be able to run your finger under the straps, but the cat should not be able to wiggle out of the harness.

The first official "walk" should be indoors with the cat just dragging the leash behind him on the floor (and likely playing with it.) Don't be surprised if your cat plops down on his side and looks at you as if to say, "This thing weighs a ton!" Work with the Tuxedo in short 10-15 minute lessons until he pays no attention to the leash. Then and only then pick the lead up and follow the cat around.

That distinction is the primary difference between walking a dog and being walked by a cat. The leash is there so you have a way to prevent the cat from escaping and minimally controlling where he goes.

For the most part if you really want to initiate a course change, you'll have to pick the cat up. You'll be letting your Tuxedo explore the yard with you in tow, not the other way around.

With young cats, the process is much easier and shorter, but even older cats can be taught to walk on a leash. If an older cat has spent the majority of its time indoors, he will be nervous when he goes outside on his leash for the first time.

Stay close by and speak soothingly to your pet. In no time his native curiosity will have taken over and he'll think the whole business of harness and leash is the best idea he's ever had.

Teaching Your Cat Commands

Tuxedos have shown an excellent capacity to amass a working vocabulary and to respond to "commands." Any time you are attempting to teach your cat a "trick" or to elicit a desired response, cater to the cat's natural inclinations.

If, for instance, your cat is naturally given to using his paws, it's much easier to get him to touch an object in return for a treat and to increase the complexity of the behavior over time. Your Tuxedo will quickly catch on that a game is involved, and go along with you.

Limit any "lessons" to less than 15 minutes, and always reward your cat with treats as well as praise. Many people say that cats do not respond to verbal affirmations, but this isn't true of people cats like Tuxedos.

Tuxedo cats are pleased to please you and will try to be even more agreeable when their response garner lots of love and attention for their efforts. (Bear in mind that this desire to please doesn't prevent a cat from completely ignoring you when you're unhappy with him.)

Cats can hear sounds at great distances. They can pinpoint the origin of a noise to within 3 inches (7.5 cm) of its exact location at a distance of one yard (91 cm) in under 6/100ths of a second.

You'll do much better getting your cat's attention by speaking softly rather than using the kind of "command voice" to which a dog would respond. Whispering gets your cat's attention far faster than "barking" at him.

A cat's hearing is roughly twice as good as ours. Humans hear in a range of 20-23 kHz, while cats pick up frequencies from 45-65 kHz.

One of the reasons cats often ignore men, especially those with deep voices, is that the speech may actually fall below the cat's normal "radar," which is pitched for high sounds, like the squeaking of a mouse.

Choose command words with clear, distinct syllables and try to pair verbal commands with visual cues. Cats communicate with one another via an elaborate system of body langue.

You can tell a cat to get "down" off the counter, but he's more likely to learn the meaning of your emphatically downward pointing finger and read the displeasure in your expression.

Selecting Toys

As for toys, Tuxedos are excellent jumpers. Any toys that elicit chasing, running, and jumping, are perfect choices.

Dangling toys on wands that allow your Tuxedo to jump and swat and keep you out of harm's way of extended claws cost $8-$10 (£5-£7).

Remember that these are "with supervision only" toys. You need to be present and part of the game. Otherwise the string can be a choking hazard.

(Note that both string and Christmas tinsel also raise the potential for intestinal blockages if swallowed. These items can become twisted in the intestine and must be surgically removed. Be very, very careful in allowing your cat access to string.)

Beyond that, it's really just a matter of learning your cat's tastes. It's always good to have some toys that will stimulate your Tuxedo's interest whether you're around to join in or not.

One sure hit is some variation of a half-closed ring or tube with a ball inside. Cats will try for hours to chase the ball and get it out of the enclosure. (They won't be successful; these units are very sturdy and therefore safe toys.)

As an example, the Petmate Crazy Circle Interactive Cat Toy (which comes in both large and small sizes) retails for $10-$12 / £6-£8.

"Crinkle" sacks and tunnels are also a huge hit because they not only provide a place to hide and watch, but also make a pleasing amount of racket when kitty goes rocketing through. (Note this is one toy you'll likely want to put up before bedtime so you can get some sleep!)

The SmartyKatCrackleChute Tunnel Cat Toy, which has a 9.5 inch / 24.13 cm opening and is 35 inches / 88.9 cm long retails for $10 / £6.

(Remember to never leave your Tuxedo alone with toys that have small detachable parts or lengths of string or ribbon. All represent choking or blockage hazards if swallowed.)

Opt for Larger Scratching "Trees"

You'll definitely want not just a scratching post, but an actually "tree" for these agile beauties. Putting a price range to scratching equipment is more difficult. The traditional carpeted pole will cost around $30 (£20).

Elaborate cat "trees" with perches, tunnels, and other hiding places can range anywhere from $100 (£65) to $300 (£197) and up.

If your Tuxedo does begin to attack the furniture, consider using herbal or adhesive scratching deterrents. Cats have an aversion to both pennyroyal or orange essence, which can be used to drive them off a favorite piece of furniture. You'll pay $12-$15 / £8-£10 for spray bottles of these mixtures.

Cats also dislike anything that feels tacky to their paws, which has led to the development of double-sided adhesive solutions to discourage scratching. These items retail for about $8-$10 / £5-$7.

Your Tuxedo's Grooming Needs

Even with their heavy triple coat, a Tuxedo Cat requires only minimal grooming. They are affected by the change in season, so you will see increased shedding in the spring, as the weather is getting warmer.

Otherwise, regular combing and brushing is all that's needed to stimulate the cat's skin, and to keep the coat healthy and clean. Select a wire-toothed comb that will reach down to the skin, but that will not pull at the hair.

A "pin cushion" brush (widely spaced individual bristles on a rubber base) is a better choice than a "slicker" brush. This kind of tool efficiently removes loose hair, and doesn't run the risk of damaging the cat's skin.

Pin cushion brushes retail for $7-$10 (£5-£7), and wire-toothed combs for $10-$12 (£7-£8).

Tuxedos are not prone to mat or tangle, but if that does become an issue for any reason, you will want to consult with a professional groomer or with your vet to safely shave away or remove the mats.

A cat's skin is extremely fragile. DO NOT attempt to cut mats out on your own. You can seriously injure your pet.

Chapter Twelve: Tuxedo Cat Health

Overall, Tuxedo Cats are a reasonably healthy breed, but like all cats, they need your vigilant attention to provide the preventive care they can't give themselves. An attentive owner is the best health "insurance" any cat can have.

Spaying and Neutering

The vast majority of purebred Tuxedo cats that are sold by catteries are "pet quality." This means that, in relation to the accepted breed standard, the cat has some minor perceived flaw that prevents it from either being shown or used in a breeding program.

Such "flaws" are all but invisible to the thrilled new owner who is delighted to welcome a personable, devoted Tuxedo into their life.

However, spaying and neutering will be required as a condition of the adoption, since breeders are constantly attempting to improve the quality of their bloodlines and of the breed as a whole

Typically, the agreement stipulates that spaying and neutering must occur before the cat reaches six months of age, and that proof be forwarded to the cattery that the procedure has been performed.

Working with your veterinarian, there should be no problem meeting this requirement, since medically, this is the optimal timeframe for the surgeries to occur.

Although costs will always vary by specific clinic, there are inexpensive options for these surgeries in the range of $50 (£30).

Since spaying and neutering are the first medical procedures your cat will require apart from vaccinations, however, this is a good time to consider establishing a long-term relationship with a veterinarian.

Establishing a Relationship with a Veterinarian

With the high cost of just about everything today, everyone is in the position of attempting to save money. Having just paid for a purebred cat, many people have some degree of "sticker shock" and have an impulse to try to minimize the expense of spaying or neutering. That may not be the best option, however.

Most cat owners prefer to work with one veterinarian over the course of a cat's life if at all possible. This not only allows all the animal's records to be amassed in one location by one medical professional, but it creates a situation where your vet will know and completely understand your cat's health.

Spending a little more in the beginning to work with a vet in whom you can invest your long-term confidence is money well spent.

Program of Vaccinations

Vaccinations have been instrumental over the last two decades in dramatically reducing contagious disease transmission in companion animals.

At the same time, however, there has been some controversy about the potential for tumors arising at the site of the injections.

If this is an area of concern for you, discuss the vaccination process with your veterinarian so that you fully understand the purpose of each injection.

At the time, you adopt your Tuxedo kitten, you will be given a record of any shots the baby has already received, and an indication of when the next "boosters" are to be given.

A normal program of vaccinations includes:

- Distemper combo

This shot is first administered at 6 weeks of age, with repeat vaccinations on a 3-4-week schedule until the kitten is 16 months old. A booster is then given at one year of age, and others at three-year intervals for the remainder of your Tuxedo cat's life.

The disease against which this "combo" provides defense are: panleukopenia (FPV or feline infectious enteritis), rhinotracheitis (FVR, an upper respiratory / pulmonary infection), and calicivirus (causes respiratory infections).

The vaccine may also include protection against chlamydophilia, which causes conjunctivitis.

- Feline leukemia

This injection is given at 2 months of age, and repeated 3 to 4 weeks later. At one year of age, your Tuxedo cat will receive a booster, with annual injections thereafter.

- Rabies

Rabies vaccinations are administered according to local law, typically on an annual basis with some type of legal proof of the inoculation provided to the pet owner.

On average vaccinations are priced at around $40 (£26) per injection.

Practice Good Preventative Healthcare

Following a good program of preventive care that includes vigilant and loving monitoring of the animal's overall well-being is vital in ensuring the Tuxedo cat's long-term health.

Most people do not understand that cats have an approach to pain that is very different from our own. In their worldview, someone is always higher up on the food chain. To show pain is to open themselves to vulnerability to larger, stronger, more aggressive animals.

Consequently, cats hide their pain or ill health and can be very sick before their humans realize what is going on. It's important that you know and look for potential signs of bad health to spot a problem before it becomes serious or life threatening.

- Be aware of any changes in weight, either in terms of gains or losses. When a Tuxedo cat is at a healthy weight, you should be able to feel a pad of fat over the ribs, but still easily detect the bones underneath.
- Look for changes in how your Tuxedo cat moves and walks. Signs of a limp or of any reluctance to run or jump could be an indication of joint pain, muscle damage, or even an impinging growth under the surface.
- Watch for nasal dryness or discharge. A normal Tuxedo cat's nose is moist and clean, not dry, cracked, irritated, bleeding, or running.
- Discharge from the eyes is also a warning sign. Healthy Tuxedo cats have bright, interested, engaged eyes. The pupils should be perfectly centered, and the whites of the eyes should not be discolored. Also, there should be very few blood vessels evident in the whites.

- A Tuxedo cat's ears are prone to both irritation and parasitical infestation. Check for any sour or foul odor, and for any internal debris. The interior of the ear should be clean and smooth, not swollen and discolored. If your cat flinches when its ears are touched, a vet should examine the animal immediately.

- The gums should be pink and uniform in appearance, with clean, white teeth. Regular dental exams are a vital part of feline preventive medicine because they give the vet a chance to look for any lumps or lesions in the mouth. All cats are prone to oral cancers, which, if detected early, can be treated with a reasonable degree of success.

It's a good idea to start your Tuxedo cat on a program of dental care at a young age. It may sound insane, but most Tuxedo cats will be agreeable to having their teeth brushed.

Veterinarians carry oral hygiene kits, and will be glad to help you learn how to successfully work with your cat. The cost will be approximately $7-$10 (£4-£6) per kit.

Other preventive measures to take include:

- Monitoring your Tuxedo cat's breathing. Respirations should come more from the chest than the abdomen.

- Checking the body for any growths, masses, or bumps. (Always have these evaluated immediately)

- Watching for subtle changes in behavior. You will know your Tuxedo cat better than anyone. If you think something is not right, it probably isn't. Better to make a trip to the vet to be safe than to neglect a potential problem.

Watch for Changes in Litter Box Behavior

The number one cited reason for cats being given up to shelters is some form of inappropriate elimination.

If your cat misses, or goes outside the box, the first thing you must do is get the animal to the vet. Your cat may very well have an undiagnosed or chronic kidney or bladder infection.

In feline logic, if trying to go in the box hurts, they'll try to go somewhere else. They associate the box with the pain, and try to escape it.

Barring a health concern, your cat may not like its litter or litter box or, frankly, you may be the real problem.

Cats are very tidy creatures. If their box is not well-maintained and scooped daily, they won't want to use it. Would you want to use a disgusting bathroom?

This can also extend to replacing old boxes that have absorbed odors into the plastic of the pan.

Cats should receive a new box at least twice a year (quarterly is better). This will not only make kitty happy, but it will cut down on potential odors in your home.

Potential for Hypertrophic Cardiomyopathy

Like many purebred cats, there is a potential for Tuxedos to suffer from a thickening of the heart muscle known as hypertrophic cardiomyopathy (HCM), which is the most common heart disease among all felines.

In discussing health issues with your breeder, ask about HCM in their cattery 's bloodline. Beware of a breeder who claims their line is completely HCM free.

There is no way to guarantee against a cat developing the condition, but most breeders will be prepared to discuss whether or not the problem has surfaced in their animals.

If a breeder dodges this question, be suspicious.

It is generally best not to buy a kitten unless the cat's parents have been specifically tested for the presence of HCM via an echocardiogram.

Sadly, HCM is a prominent cause of death in many companion cats. It eventually leads to fluid in the lungs, blood clots, and heart failure.

Feline Lower Urinary Tract Disease (FLUTD)

There is now sufficient data to prove that Feline Lower Urinary Tract Disease (FLUTD) is a hereditary issue in Tuxedos.

This problem is inclusive of urinary tract infections, blockages, and kidney stones in both males and females. (The risk of blockage from lower urinary crystals is higher and more dangerous in males.)

The condition can be successfully treated with special foods and a diet that emphasizes liquids. It is imperative that any sign of urinary problems be immediately investigated since left untreated, a blockage is not only extremely painful, but potentially fatal.

(Note that there is also some evidence to suggest that Tuxedos are prone to the development of benign cysts of the kidneys due to Polycystic Kidney Disease, once thought to be a health issue exclusive to the Persian Breed.)

Chapter Thirteen: Breeding and Showing Tuxedo Cats

Making the decision to become a Tuxedo cat breeder is not as simple as getting a pair of cats and letting nature take its course. While it might be just that easy for the cats, breeding is not just an idle hobby to be taken up lightly. It's a way of life, and one much more likely to empty your pockets than to make you rich.

While it is certainly true that purebred Tuxedo kittens command a handsome price, most breeders will quite frankly tell you that for them, a good year is one in which they break even.

Money goes out of a cattery at a much faster rate than it comes in. Simply multiply the expense of caring for one cat by however many animals you intend to keep and watch the dollar signs mount.

Weigh Your Decision Carefully

Never consider becoming a Tuxedo breeder until you have fully immersed yourself in the culture surrounding catteries and cat shows. You need to meet and talk with existing breeders, either in person, or online in discussion forums.

While you can certainly find Tuxedo specific discussion forums, any site that draws together a large number of cat breeders will be instrumental in helping you make your own decision.

All breeders, regardless of the cats with which they work, share the same kinds of problems. These people, who may well become your colleagues or competitors in the future, are an invaluable source of support and information.

Only people who are consumed by the same passion for felines that should underlie the decision to open a cattery can really help you make an informed decision.

Part of that process is a matter of addressing some difficult but crucial questions.

- Can you make the commitment?

This is not just a commitment of time and money, but also of space, dedication, responsibility, and even heartache. Your nights, weekends, and holidays may no longer belong to you. Part of your home may be taken over, or an addition may be required, to adequately house and care for your animals.

You will be working with living creatures that depend on you. Some kittens won't make it. Can you take that? And can you take giving up kittens for adoption, even to carefully vetted and perfect homes? How will your family react? Will you have support or constant opposition?

- Can you work out the logistics?

This logistics involve covering the initial costs of set up, acquiring a breeding queen or stud, housing multiple cats, and making everything work in a spatial sense. That extends to what the neighbors will think, and how they may react to increased traffic on your property. (Thankfully, Tuxedos are a quiet breed.)

- Do you have a back-up, failsafe plan?

Yes, as hard as it may be to contemplate failure in the beginning, this part of your plan is crucial. What happens to your cats if it doesn't work?

- Do you have a plan for placing your animals in the event that you start a cattery and then have to shut it down in mid-operation?

Remember, the welfare of your animals is paramount, which means always thinking about the worst-case scenario while working to create the best outcome.

Work Out Estimated Costs

Be proactive about estimating your potential costs. Prices are dependent on individual circumstance, but make sure to include:

- Reference materials to understand the fine points of the Tuxedo breed and of its genetics.

- Your foundation animals. A breeding queen and/or stud or the applicable fees to pair your animals with those from another cattery.

- Repeat FIV/FELV tests for any animals that must go "visiting."

- Routine and emergency veterinary expenses including those associated with pregnancy. (Discuss all contingencies fully with the vet you will be using.)

- All additional cat furniture and toys including kittening pens and crates for transporting animals.

- Any construction costs including adding on to your home, or modifying your structure to keep intact animals separate to avoid unplanned litters of kittens.

Multiply your costs by the number of animals you will be keeping, and add on a reasonable amount for an emergency reserve.

Showing Tuxedo Cats

Generally, people who breed Tuxedo cats are also the ones who show them. Breeders are, after all, hardcore enthusiasts.

Cat shows allow them to display their animals and the excellence of their bloodlines, and an impressive list of awards lends prestige to a cattery.

This is not to say that an individual who owns a beautiful Tuxedo may not want to show that cat, but most exhibitors are also breeders.

This is one of the reasons cats' shows are such an excellent resource for people who are considering adopting a purebred cat. You won't walk out of a show with a kitten, but you can certainly walk out with a fistful of business cards.

For this reason alone, you may find yourself in the cat show environment as a spectator, and it's imperative that you understand how to behave yourself!

The Dos and Don'ts of Attending a Cat Show

Spectators at cat shows have to remember the cardinal rule. DON'T TOUCH!

That's hard to do when you're among so many beautiful animals. Try to remember that this rule is not to penalize you, but to protect the cats.

Most cat diseases are highly communicable. If you pet a cat infected with a disease and touch another cat, you've just passed along the bacteria or virus.

If you are asked to pet a cat at a show, consider it a high compliment and don't blink when the exhibitor hands you a bottle of hand sanitizer. Use it, and then enjoy the rare chance to interact with the cat.

If someone yells, "Right of way," yield. Move. Get out of the way. Or get run over! Cat shows are amazingly hectic, crowded, and busy places. When exhibitors are called to the ring, they have to get there in a limited amount of time or face disqualification.

Understand that if you're talking to an exhibitor who gets called to the ring, they will likely turn on their heel, take their cats, and leave without so much as a word. They are trusting you to know the ropes and understand that they aren't being rude. They're in a hurry.

If you are near the show ring when judging starts, stop talking and LISTEN. You do not want to do anything to distract the exhibitor or worse yet the cat, and, because judge make comments on animals while they are examining them, you'll likely learn a great deal by paying close attention.

Finally, if you hear the dreaded alarm, "LOOSE CAT," your only response should be to FREEZE. You should never try to help. Be quiet, be still, and do nothing more than signal the location of the outlaw animal should you see it.

The Mechanics of Cat Shows in Action

Cat shows are different from dog shows in a number of ways. Cats are only removed from their cages while being judged, otherwise they're kept secured at all other times.

The atmosphere is very hectic, and almost festive, with exhibitors elaborately decorating their cages and the adjacent area. In spite of all the activity, however, the actual progress of the show can be agonizingly slow.

Cats are far less receptive to being judged, and many categorically do not like the show atmosphere. Dramatic escapes are a panicked hallmark of these events.

Also, unlike dog shows, there will be a class for household pets, which is often a prime attraction for young people to become interested in the cat fancy.

The actual evaluation of the animals is done according to published breed standards formulated by the official body sponsoring the show.

The more completely an animal conforms to the points of the breed standard, the higher its score and performance in the ring.

Tuxedo Cat Care Sheet

With time, your familiarity with the nuances of caring for your Tuxedo, as well as your bond with your beloved cat, will grow. Occasionally, you may wish to reference certain information or details without having to go back through this entire book. This section is intended to help you by summarizing some of the key points you will need to know about your Tuxedo: from general information, health and grooming concerns, or in matters of breeding. Always remember, though, that the process of being a responsible cat owner is a lifetime journey of learning and growing. Use this book as a starting point, or to further your knowledge - but you will probably soon discover that the responsibilities of cat ownership entails a continuous learning process